You Are Man

You Are Man

Chadwick Norwood

Chadwick Norwood

2014

First Printing: 2014

ISBN 978-0-578-13795-7

Chadwick Norwood
PO BOX 73164
Baton Rouge, LA 70874
www.chadzmind.com

Ordering Information:

Special discounts are available on quantity purchases by corporations, associations, educators, and others. For details, contact the publisher at the above listed address.

U.S. trade bookstores and wholesalers:

Please contact Chadwick Norwood Tel: (225) 354-5280; or email chad@chadzmind.com

Dedication

This book is dedicated to my family who have enriched and empowered me in love, to my friends who have loved me in a way that no one else can and to the world with the hopes of empowering men like me.

Contents

Introduction 3

You Are Man 5

CHAPTER 1: The Back Story 8

Memory Lack...9

See Into Me...11

Troubled Bridges...13

Revelation...18

Fatherless Child...19

Livin..24

I Picked up My Violin Today 26

Insecurity...29

My "I"s 31

The Numbness..32

Chapter 2: Sensual 34

Hold Me...35

Early Monday 37

Feel Again 39

Shade...40

Flames 41

Bath Time...42

Wet Realities..44

A Changed Hoe 46

Chapter 3: Want to Love.................................47

Longing 48

Lonely..50

So Far..52

Dear Moderation..53

Sparkle 55

Think About You Every Night 56

Sometimes 57

Chapter 4: The Love Stories..**59**

First Date..60

Second Date 61

Letter One 62

Rescue 63

Letter Two 64

No Flaws 65

Letter Three 67

In Your Own Time 68

Similarities 69

25..73

Letter Four 75

Chapter 5: Break-Up..**77**

Your Time With Me Is Up..78

Waves 80

Self Portrait...81

Your Promises..82

Your Paint, Your Brush 84

Lust Letter 87

Lessons Learned from Dogs...88

Sense 90

I Abstain...91

Chapter 6: Rebuild **93**

One day 94

Ready For Love?...96

I Washed It Off 99

Clean-up 103

Pruned 106

Introduction

You Are Man is a collection of my poems, letters and thoughts. Looking back over my life, I have had both beautiful and ugly moments. I can remember being teased as a child because I was not like the other boys. I always wanted to jump rope and play volleyball instead of playing flag football. I excelled in music and arts but failed tragically whenever I played sports.

As an adult, I tend not to follow the trends of dress and grooming that most men followed. Pink is my favorite color. I have arched my eyebrows for so long that I do not know what my natural eyebrows look like anymore. I wear my pants and clothes in my size so they fit. For a phase in my life, it did not matter if the numerical size was a thirty-eight or a sixteen. I do not get caught up by numbers.

Before I even had "manhood", it was threatened. I was teased because my speaking voice has never been lower than mezzo alto. In fact, my voice did not change until I was maybe twenty-one years old. My sense of color coordination and selection has always rivaled other men around me. It proves itself to be a bit much for corporate America at times. I am always told I can stand to tone it down a bit by men, but women love it.

I have always had too much personality to fit into the traditional definition of manhood. Because I do not fit, does it then make me anything other than a man? Does it make me less than a man? I have felt so many emotions, but nothing has affected me as deeply as the possibility that the answer to this question could be yes.

I have as many emotions and degrees of emotions as there are colors and hues and cried enough tears to fill the Grand Canyon twice over, yet I still am a man. If my expression was a color, it would be a hot pink, electricity charged enigma, yet I am still a man.

This book is dedicated to the people whose struggle resembles mine. It is my hope to inspire conversations about love, life and relationships by sharing the words I have felt through my most difficult of times. Being vulnerable in truth can feel like inadequacy. Never be afraid to say how you truly feel. You are man, no matter what the world says.

You Are Man

You believe in your dream

Though the roads to fulfillment are crowded with trees,

Littered with the trash of disappointment,

Flooded with the waters of confusion,

And you are blown left and right by the winds of opposition

But you believe anyway

That one day you will find reciprocation

Gratification

And justification for the hard life you have been given

Vindication from all of your foes

Victory over all past loves gone wrong

And healing to the scars of years old

Though the odds are against you,

You still believe

Strong, Beautiful, Loving and Compassionate

You...... are man.

You believe in your fantasy

Though tangible traces of it only exist in your mind

But not in your mind only

It exists in the minds of all,

But is covered by clouds of superficiality

Buried beneath mountains of insecurity

Petrified by years of being covered by stones

Yet, it still exists

And one day, what is buried will come to life

And live out the purpose of its presence

Its soul exists because your soul exists

It exists to supplement the efforts of one to be made whole

And to compliment your life

And exist with your soul

And together you will continue through the tests of life

And be nothing less than successful

Strong, Beautiful, Loving and Compassionate

You...... are man.

CHAPTER 1: The Back Story

Every ordinary man has an even greater story that is often never told publicly. It is often a story of tragedy to triumph. If ever spoken, it is spoken in whispers that only few can hear. If it is ever acted out, it is often in actions that others do not understand.

My story is filled with memories of things I have buried so deep that I often forget them. When memories resurface, I experience them with the same intensity as when they happened. Most would say that I do not have the ability to just move forward or that I am holding on to the past. I disagree. Sometimes, revisiting a place can bring someone else who is still there.

Mental bondage is the worst kind of slavery. If going back one thousand times would save one, then I will take the trips.

Memory Lack

I don't really know when I decided to stop having a memory

I can imagine (if I remember correctly) that it was my second year of college

At that point, I was in a failed relationship (I think)

I got cheated on with some guy named James or Jay (something like that)

Then I began to delve into my not so hidden desire for the same sex

Only to find out men sucked too

I began to stress myself out

I might have had a few anxiety attacks

Developed bad eating habits

And as I recall, became very self conscious

Completely gave up on life

Or did I give up after the recurring nightmares?

I asked God to wipe my mind clean

Erase my hard drive and empty the recycling bin

I said something like, "Lord, please erase my memory, I do not want to remember anything bad that has happened to me. I cannot take it"

....and I'll be God-blessed

I think he did it

Now I sit and wonder if that was really a good prayer to pray

(or if I prayed it at all)

Am I truly done with my past?

I don't know... but I do know this

I CAN'T REMEMBER NOTHING

See Into Me

I don't want you to see through me

I want you to see into me

See the clouds of complexity

And understand that they only rain when they've been filled with too much

See the hurricanes and the storm front as it rages

For only then can you gain permanent status in the calm

See the lies and misrepresentations I've seen in my eyes,

And you'll see why I cry when the truth is so real and why seeing love moves me

Look into my ears and read the writing on the walls of them

For only then will you understand the passion of my speech

Look at my heart and see that it has been detached from others and now repaired, mended and healed

For only then can you understand it is hard enough for me to live for me

.....Much less live for you...

See into me

Because if you see through me, you won't understand me

I need you to understand me and not just deal with me

...That is the only way you'll appreciate me.

Troubled Bridges

(DEDICATED TO MY DEPARTED FRIEND)

What happens to the pain I hide?

Time and time again,

I have tried to hide it behind smiles

And covered misery I feel with wiles

pitted at all that despise me and speak my detriment,

I have adorned myself with jewelry, rings

And the king's habiliments

And built walls upon walls of sarcasm

So that I not only appear to be made of steel

But also look flawless and stainless

Just to look the part for high judges in low places

In hopes that they will spare me of your cruel words

And the utterances of ignorance

For you don't truly know of what you are speaking

What you see is merely my response

To the raging waters I see on the inside of me

And the internal turmoil that leave me torn

And feeling totally unloved

Longing to be loved

My bloodline fights a losing battle daily

While my extended bloodline acts as though they have lost me

They see me but act as if they can't find me

Once found

In shame, they try to hide me

Their daily decisions are regulated by looks on other people's faces

By high judges in low places

That speak ill of me in the name of righteousness

And blaming their fear and hate of me on their religion

And none of them can see what is truly going on the inside of me

I feel like I am walking through life barefoot

But I have to do it with poise and grace

Over grounds covered with burning glass, brimstone and hot ash

...I only seek something soothing before I am consumed

Feeling like my dilemma is doubled

Like a candle rapidly burning at both ends

And winds are causing waves higher than I have ever seen

The waters below me are in turmoil

And the bridge I am crossing is troubled

What happens to pain that won't subside?

I have given divinity from my loins to many

In hopes that the joining of spirits will heal it

I have tried to drown the pain repeatedly with wine and spirits

Saturated and inundated it with smoke from anything that would produce smoke in efforts to deoxygenate it so that it would die...

I have gotten so high that I mounted with eagles wings

And ascended into the sky until mountains appeared as molecules

I have given my whole heart to so many that it is numerically uncountable

And made myself available to the needs and thoughts of others so much

That I forgot to see my own necessities

Left to realize that the walls in my temple have been defiled

The essence of the things that make me individually me

Are now gone away from me

Some given

Some taken

And now knowing that I was mistaken

That giving away the fruits of my flesh was never the answer

That numbing the pain with worldly spirits only caused pain to spread faster

And bleed more hastily

And now I lie here filled with tainted thoughts

Tainted vision

And tainted blood

Tainted

And tired

Feeling like I am walking through life barefoot

And to keep from being criticized

I have to glide along with poise and grace

Over grounds covered with burning glass, brimstone and hot ash

I only seek something soothing before I am consumed by fire

Feeling like my dilemma is doubled

Like a candle rapidly burning at both ends

And winds are causing waves higher than I have ever seen

The waters below me are in turmoil

And the bridge I am crossing is troubled

Fire destroys

And rather than be burned into a mound of unrecognizable ash,

The cooling waters that I once feared will baptize me

And remove the impurities that both you and I have placed on me

For water cleanses

And I only long to be clean

Revelation

Every time a "friend" hurts you, they kill a dream... Kill a hope... Kill a portion of the love you have for them... AND kill a piece of the positive energy that you have set aside for them. In anything living, once the energy is gone it is essentially dead. How much energy can you place into others   before   you   feel   dead?

With this realization, I am done with letting people kill the positivity and love in me. Instead I am going to let the positivity be transferred into the PEOPLE who put positive   energy   back   into   me.

Cain deceived his brother by misrepresentation of motives, killed (took energy from) his brother and THEN lied about it to God. What makes me any different?

LIFE LESSON: Keep no space for liars. They will deceive you by misrepresenting their intentions, kill you and your positivity and deny their wrongdoings to their gods, man and God. God will hear your cries.... But WHEREVER and WHENEVER possible... Don't cry if you don't have to... And don't die.

Fatherless Child

Though I'm not... I am...

They say I was created in love

One man.. one woman...

Ovulation.. ejaculation....

Out of MILLIONS, I am created by one sperm infiltrating one egg...

Created one me.. who came into this world with 10 toes...

twelve fingers (I've always been a little different)

and a head FULL of hair (how things change....)

..but somewhere along the line half of the love used to create me changed focus..

I've been told stories about how when I was a baby that the man would ensure I had the necessities to be nourished and that I never went hungry...

But as an adult, I have longed to be fed the wisdom of a man from the man that created half of me...

Though often times I feel he half created me...

Just as a seed planted by a farmer

It is routine to water them the first time so that the seed can begin to grow into form..

But without dedication to ensure its survival...

The seed is left to get what it needs from the elements to continue growing its roots..

And with a little help from nature it will sprout out of the ground and form a stem..

And under the light of the sun.. photosynthesis will naturally occur and it will grow into maturity...

But... If the farmer had just come around and gave the seeds a little fertilizer frequently

Then maybe the plant would have grown to be stronger

In short y'all... I didn't get the shit I needed from him to make me stronger..

I had to learn how to be a man from women

Though I would never disregard the impartation from the man who stepped in when he stepped out, but with children of his own... How much would be fair of him to give to me?

So sometimes... I feel like a fatherless child.....

Though I am not... I am...

I've been told stories about how when I was a baby that the man would bring me pampers....

But as an adult, I cannot remember ever being pampered by the man..

A child on a tricycle.. I was told about how the man SAVED me from being killed by an oncoming car when I wasn't paying attention...

And how when I would see him across the street I would RUN to him without looking both ways to ensure safety because as a child I had the thought then that if I just made it to the man... I'd be okay....

But now I can't see him across the street.. I can't see him anywhere..

Just as sheep left with no shepherd

They wander about aimlessly

And without the security of the shepherd

the sheep are left as prey for the wolves...

Without the wisdom of the shepherd..

The sheep are dumb with no guidance..

left to survive with their own thoughts...

Using the deaths of the sheep around them to learn instincts on how not to be killed....

In short... left to die....

So sometimes... I feel like a fatherless child.....

Though I am not... I am...

He disappeared... providing no support.. no guidance....

so when you tell me that I am supposed to believe that I have a father in heaven.. I am confused..

and when you tell me "Let thy will be done on earth as it is in heaven"

I often wonder if I am destined to not be loved and it is the will that I feel this way.....

How am I to believe that a father I can't see, touch or feel can provide for me

When the father that I should be able to see does not...

How am I to believe that the creator of the world has something special for me..

somewhere..

That he is with me every step of the way..

That I am created in his image so when I look at myself.... I should see love....

When the father whose blood runs through my veins,

And Whose features I share doesn't give love to me...

So sometimes when I look at myself.. I don't see love..

I don't see the king in me that I am supposed to see....

I see someone searching for what I have not received

and in disbelief that I could have it from a father in heaven without first receiving it form a father on earth....

some people say... children are created in love.....

I challenge me to believe that children were created BY love......

I look into the mirror with tears in my eyes and tell myself that I am special to my father in heaven

Even if the father on earth shows me otherwise....

The creator of my soul loves it...

Even if the donator of my good looks doesn't show it.....

Sometimes I feel like a fatherless child...

Though it seems like I am....... I now know I am not..

Livin

I don't know where the hell I'm livin

People jus stealin and aint nobody givin

The only peace is the piece....

Plant hate seeds and you'll grow hate trees...

No more mediation.. Just retaliation..

Insulting has become a sport that's done for fun...

Lyrical onslaughts of insults on a fly beat now can be number one song...

....All the while not really sayin shit....Toilet...

Babies having babies

Babies killing babies

All because we've stopped nurturing babies...

Baby got to grow up fast...

Dingalings growing straight to dicks

Booties growing straight to azz....

We done stop raising ladies and gentlemen

And started teaching our kids to become niggaz and bitches

.....Because das real and the only way you going to make it on the battlefield....

Fuck you some bitches and then you become a man

Fuck that nigga and get all of his money you can

Because that is the master plan apparently...

My car stereo done got popped 3 times so I don't leave my face on..

I don't leave home without my game face on...

Because undoubtedly.....

Imma run into someone born in hate..

Raised in ignorance

And reassured that it's okay to be nothing.......

And do nothing..

But have the audacity to see me and want to say something...

I don't know where I'm livin..

I Picked up My Violin Today

I keep it hidden under my bed

not near the foot of the bed where people might be able to see it under the bed skirt as they pass by...

Oh no!

I keep it up near the head of the bed

Behind all the other boxes and bundles

Deep in the shadows

firmly tucked standing against the wall in its case.

so that for even for me, it is a test to find it.

Now, I, perplexed by a sudden change in life

It is like...

Almost everything I have known to be true, now untrue

Everything, I believed to be endless, now paused

I pray and pray for answers with very few given, but by men I am told...

"Chad, you should find self"

Who is self?

For the longest, I had been taught that self was something I should deny and avoid so that there would be greater glory in the end....

Should I find the self that was haunted by nightmares about being molested as a child?

Troubled by the question of was it REALLY molestation...or was it participation??

The same self that at first caused me to despise people touching me,

Then changed to letting everybody who's anybody (or nobody) touch me...

Only gratified and satisfied by pain...

Because I felt that I needed to be punished and chastised until my face was completely covered with tears from my eyes.....

Finally left unsatisfied and confused...

Not knowing if my everyday life and desires revolve around that one incident..

Picking up my violin reminded me of the times when I had to use it as a weapon to defend myself against people who offended me....

Times when I could be found in a ditch beat up after getting off of the bus for reasons I cannot even remember

Maybe... that was the self that had WAYY too much mouth and not enough hands

Should I be the self who has learned to be a master swordsman with words?

A weapon serves two purposes: to injure others and to protect self

Once I opened the case

I stared at it and remembered the beautiful harmonies that would flow from it

I'm also reminded of the dissonance

I picked up my violin today, but could not bring myself to   play   it.

Insecurity

I find it sometimes much easier to lurk in the shadows

Not being seen, but always sensed

Making just enough noise to let you know that I am there

Not being able to be predicted as to when I will creep out and attack

I find it easier to hide in gray clouds way up in the sky

So that people will wonder if I will pour out my insides and drown all they treasure

Make people bring out their umbrellas in preparation for what may come

And though the weatherman predicted his percentages of what's likely to come

There is no true certainty

Sometimes

I like to clap like thunder and make lighting flash just to scare the hell outcha ass

But most times, I like to drift on

And never pour out who I am

Partially because I don't want you to know anything about me but the me I want you to see

I am a little scared of critique and judgment

I have seen enough people fighting in Parliament to win favors of royalty

Only to rub noses with the richest and kiss the hand of worldly royalty

All while not being themselves authentically

My "I"s

Sometimes I don't have I's

And it is then that I am the most beautiful of God's creations

So confident in vainglory

I am invincible, unbeatable and filled with unshakeable personal fait

It is in those moments that life is all about me

But sometimes my I's come out

And then ironically it becomes impossible for me to see anything I once saw before

I doubt beauty

I doubt self worth and feel like I can't do anything

I hate my I's.

The Numbness

my mind is a blank canvas

no thoughts.. and even if it were to paint something..

I wouldn't be able to see it because my eyes just stay closed

everything tastes the same

from chicken to peppermints

all the same.. nothing different

liquor don't even get me drunk no more.. just sleepy

I don't dance no more

I still smile though... sporadically..

just walking around blank-faceded (if there is such a thing)

it is almost like I am living with no feeling

well.. not almost like.. I am living with no feeling

I am sitting trying to remember what it was like to feel

Chapter 2: Sensual

The nature of a man is to dominate in all things. However, there comes a time when every man lets down his guard and allows others to take the lead. It is in those moments that the man is truly beautiful and senses are at their highest. In those moments, he is in tune with the world and focused on being authentic because the need to appear strong is erased.

There is a fine line between sensual and sexual. As a man, it is easy to lean more toward the sexual side of being because orgasms produce something visual. However, the experience of the body extends far beyond something you can see. After many failed experiences with trying to have one or the other, I have learned to love living life on the line between the two (with one foot on either side of the line).

True satisfaction lives in experiencing life in all the senses....

Hold Me

Something magnetic pulls me to you and I can't move when you hold me

Time just don't feel like time

Is it passing by when you hold me?

I don't have an agenda

You are the only thing I want to be into when you hold me

Reality don't seem real to me when you hold me

Sometimes I rush to do things I got to do in a day so you can hold me

I forget about the dumb shit you say when you hold me

Your arms are my ticket away

Help me pack my bags tonight

I don't want to stay here

PLEASE hold me....

Sometimes it is the small things like fingertips that get me...

I swear my body has your ridge detail memorized

and if I was dusted for fingerprints...

I would only hope that the patterns left on my skin would leave one mesmerized.

Create constellations on my skin like it is your sky

Write your name on my chest like my body is sand

Let the waves come and wash it away so you can do it all again

Early Monday

Just standing here in your bathroom

Looking at my crust-filled eyes

The touch and feel of cotton in my mouth

Hands just as dry, with ashy arms and feet

But despite all of this I feel beautiful

.... for my body glistens

and it gleams with precious stones and gems

Preciously placed on me...

I see Jasper...

And a few Amethysts...

Innumerable red-colored Rubies....

With polished Rose quartz

Polished Onyx

And Diamonds that just shine

Just standing here in awe of myself

In shear amazement..

With the shower running

My moving... hesitant..

I have to get ready to go to work...

And... Cleanliness is a priority,

But... How I feel and what I see is so beautiful to me

And... I don't want to wash it off.

Feel Again

I need you to forgive my eyes.

It has been such a long time since they've seen a sight so amazing

So   they   are   staring   and   gazing
Please forgive my lips

They quiver just a bit when you kiss them

I can't recall feeling touches this tender,

And if I have, then I don't remember

Please forgive the nervous energy

I know you feel when you put your hands on me

My sensory does flips when you touch me with your fingertips

Please be patient

My hips will match your syncopation

I promise to make this a night to remember

Just wait until I find my rhythm

Touch me

Hold me

Teach me how to feel again

Shade

Been so long since I've felt like this...totally helpless...

I like to be in control, but when you touch my skin

I lose my only defense..

Only you baby can make this feel so right

And only you can beat me when I try to fight

Only your touch can make me feel so safe

And only you can bring the sunshine to my shade.......

Spend my time pretending to be strong....

Just looking out for me

But then you look into my eyes.... and I know you see

For you I'm really weak

Only you baby can make this feel so right

And only you can find it when it tries to hide...

Only your touch can make this feel this great...

And only you can bring the sunshine to my shade....

Flames

My physical being is engulfed in flames

Heat radiating from my body

I need you touch me so I can feel it in the palms of your hands

Can you touch me with your lips?

I want you to feel my skin buckle between them

Chastise me with thousands of lashes of your tongue

Whip me

The moistness like gasoline

Burn me into ashes until I dissipate and am blown away

Make it feel good to me....

Please...

Bath Time

Last night I was feeling me

Me… feeling me..

I drew my bath and filled it with bath beads and oils

Found my lighter to burn some incense

And a candle

Let a little music play

I want to relax my body and chill

I took off my shirt

Shorts

Socks

Underwear

And slithered into a sea of warm goodness

Music made love to and soothed the nerve endings in my mind

While the scents of incense and vanilla infiltrated my senses

I was feeling wayyy too good y'all

Far too good to begin what I got in the tub to do

But I grabbed the soap anyway

Lathered it all over me

......then my mind clicked and it was no longer me touching me

.... It was you embracing me with you

Massaging my neck with your fingertips

I can feel you meandering and perusing the pathways of my body

Elevating every sensory element I have within me

As you caress my raised legs one by one

You migrate to my thighs and massage

Left then right

And your hands disappear into the sea

As you get a firm grasp on my masculinity,

I can feel the waves splash

And splash

And splash

...then splash and flash... you disappear

And I'm now alone again...

Me.... Feeling me....

Wet Realities

A myriad of colors, textures and tones

Form this live, moving portrait of our bodies entangled in ecstasy..

Visions and feelings...

Though faceless, I know it's your body

Because the feeling is all too familiar to me

Every hair of your chest is pressed against my chest

One hand caressing every crevice and every fold

And fondle

And embrace

And then... the hair of your face presses my face

And your hands begin their journey..

Down south to my dairy to milk me...

Stroking me from tip to base

Tip to base.. and then base to tip

I write Ooo with the motions of my hips

And grind onto you.. and grasp onto you

While grinding on you, I open my eyes

Only to realize that it's a pillow between my thighs

And I am alone

Sweating...and panting..

If and only if you were really beside me

To gratify me..

To extinguish the fire for you that has long since been burning inside of me

To put an end to my yearning for you...

If only you were by me

I would let you do what you want to do to me until I lose all sense of pride

...and all sense of feeling....... And all sense

Just pure, unadulterated sexual nonsense...

Until the sockets lose connection with the back of my eyes....

Until my body is completely overworked

And the thought of stopping is the only thing that hurts...

Drill to find oil

Churn to make cream

Come over

Let's make this a wet reality... not just a wet dream

A Changed Hoe

I am so tired of fucking

I want to get love made to me

Plainly... missionary if necessary

So much secretions and ejaculations

It will last me a lifetime

Been hot, sweaty, then alone afterwards that I will be just fine without it

I've stroked and been stroked so much that I got this shit streamlined

But in moving forward,

I never wished I could rewind

Chapter 3: Want to Love

There comes a time in every man's life that he wants to feel something deeper. Love to me is the best thing that anyone can ever feel. When authentic, it is the cure to the hurt that ails us. When genuine, it is the warmth to the hate that keeps our hearts frozen. The search to find it can lead down many roads that turn out to be dead ends. Some roads will get you closer than others, but the key to success in finding it is the desire to get there.

Do not lose momentum.

Longing

I have stretched out my petals and leaves in the manner of flowers and trees towards it.....

I have reached down, deep into the ground in the path of roots long before anchored in an attempt to anchor myself deeper into it....

I have rubbed my waterproof body against the rocks of the earth in the manner of a snake...

to exfoliate my dead, shedding skin so I can be beautiful for it.

I cannot think of any alternative methods to get it...

Don't want no alternatives for it...

When I get it, I'll know it...

I'm longing...

Longing to be loved.

Once I thought I smelt it,

But its scent, though vagrant, evaded me

I've dusted every square micrometer of my outer and inner man for its fingerprints,

but evidence has proven that it's never touched me

I've used telescopes upon telescopes to gaze eons upon light years away

in hopes that I could at least get one glimpse of it....

for at its first sight, I'd stretch out my arms to touch it.

But not even when I looked under microscopes into microbes did itself show.

Can't think of anywhere else I can look for it,

Evidence of things not seen, substance of things I hope for..

I'm longing...

Longing to be loved.

Lonely

It used to scare me...

I have always preferred to experience the day alone,

but sleeping alone at night was the worst thing

Ya see, I needed another person breathing to help move the air...

I needed another heartbeat to lull me subconsciously to sleep...

I needed skin other than mine to touch mine....

to create sensual spurts of sensory intermittently throughout the night...

I needed a different scent on my sheets so I could smell something other than me...

I learn, that my emotions are muscles

The more I work them, the stronger they get..

Lonely don't bother me all that much

as it has become the norm...

but I had no idea that you felt the same way as me...

if I did, maybe you could become the norm.....

and we can lie together and listen to each other breathe,

listen to each other's pulse quicken and settle.....

allow our skins to touch intermittently.. continually... persistently..

and create different scents on my sheets to smell...

It will be then, that I can give metaphoric muscles a much needed rest...

and we can feel un-lonely together..

but you got to be authentically you

let know what you want to do.

So Far

Lying here trying to get my breathing right, because maybe if I do

I can exhale some of this heat...

Sing a peaceful lullaby...

And inhale some sleep...

But it seems that my body is doing its own thing.....

My mind is filled with thoughts of your thing...

And the only fix I can see for my breathing is to make it match yours

And the sensation of your skin pressed onto and into me

Is the only thing that will make me exhale heat..

I am sure...

And the only lullabies I need are the moans groans of we enjoying we...

Non-poetically and non-metaphorically speaking...

I want you to touch me.....

But why you got to be so far away from me?

Dear Moderation

In moderation, we embrace and grace each other's presence...

You read my mood... I read your mood

We vibe in a way that has long since graced my life....

Most times, I fight my thoughts of you

While working late at night....

Most times, I can still smell you on me

Which makes it hard to fight....

So I find myself thinking about how crazy you are

And I smile even harder when I think about how well you fit me

How well I know we would be if we were a we

officially...... but

 In moderation, I inch along in this race

And so that I don't lose you,

I concentrated   on   enjoying   each   interesting demonstration

And not focusing on its destination.....

I know that you are not promised to me

Neither is tomorrow for that matter,

But I still look forward to talking to you then...

There just aren't enough seconds in a minute and the hours could use a few more minutes if you ask me...

If it were up to me and not to my pride,

I would tell you all my feelings and disrobe verbally

... ha... when I am not disrobed physically....

So I can feed you a full meal of my truths

Instead of allowing you to sample it in phrases and analogies...

How our special rendezvous are the highlight of my week

How you never get penciled in.... only in pen

How.... ultimately... you are the only one I see..

And I would love to see more of you

but in moderation....

I'm going let this age like fine chardonnay

Careful not to let it be like smoke in the wind and drift away...

Moderately..... show you that I can be down.....

Infatuated softly,

-Chad

Sparkle

Stay in my eyes...

Stay in my sight...

Having you in my vision has helped me envision me..

It has shined light on who I was...

Brought me into truths that I would've never known...

.. and shown me how beautiful and talented I still am...

and what I truly can be..

I'll always think about you...

Every time I sing thoughts of you will flow in the waves of my vibrato...

Every time I look at the sky, I'll see stars, and pray for your well-being...

and wish...

That in this phase in my life, I had the nerve to confess....

I love you....

but for now..

I'll just let you shine for me internally...

Since you won't be in my eyes...

and you won't be in my sight....

Think About You Every Night

I know it's a crazy time to think about someone, but you are heavily on my mind.

I imagine you sleeping with your mouth semi-closed

In a semi-fetal, semi-spooning position

Creating the perfect body shape for me to be right beside you with my arms around you

Holding you and practicing my new skill of world ignoring.

You look good even while snoring

And as I lay here,

My imagination makes my breathing match the breathing I imagine you to have

And the contractions of my heartbeats are driven to match the rhythmic vibrations of your heart that my skin feels from your body....

All in an attempt to ensure that our blood flows at the same pace..

So I can feel how you feel

And maybe... I can dream what I hope you dream...

One day... Really laying beside me....

Sometimes

Sometimes, I want to breathe and not be witness to evidence of other living things....

Sometimes, uninterrupted silence is required to process my thoughts...

Sometimes, I want to laugh with my friends with no pressure of being impressive....

Sometimes, I want to wear my comfy outfit and look like shit...

Sometimes, I want to behold the beauty of my surroundings selfishly....

Sometimes, I want to spend my money on things I like for me...

Sometimes, I want to remind me of how wonderful I am to be me and it be considered normalcy and not vanity

Sometimes, I want to feel how tender my skin is with my own hands....

Sometimes, I want to buckle under the pressure of life's demands privately...

Sometimes, I want to exist alone and behold the skies above......

And sometimes I want to love

Chapter 4: The Love Stories

Men are both easy and difficult to love. My love stories are a compilation of the many times I felt I was in love. When I am in love, I feel no fear in revealing my vulnerabilities. It is my belief that I love this way because I learned to love (and about love) from women. However, I have learned that there is nothing better in the world than a man who can honestly say how he feels and give full vent to his emotions when it comes to love.

The man's biggest challenge is to realize that vulnerability with emotions does not equal irresponsibility. In all the things that have to be juggled in a man's sphere of protection, the job of protecting emotions can seem to be neglected when loving. This turns into a battle that never seems to end. Most of my relationships have been devoured by the desire to protect emotions instead of giving them freely.

A man needs to be able to trust that his head and heart are in a safe place to love fully. Though not perfect, these are the times that I have experienced this equilibrium.

First Date

Dear Diary,

You took me out to dinner. I have always wanted to go there. I had the pasta with spinach, and it was great. He also knows that I smoke and accepts me for it which is a great relief for me. Bad habit or not, I need to smoke wherever I can and the nicotine calls.... SO.... I really like him. He introduced me to what may be my new favorite store. It has really good prices. He even bought me a new rug to put on the floor in my room. It is super cute and practical. So far, so good with this one.... He just might work.

Second Date

Not again.. not this time

This repetitive cycle catches me

I've taken every precaution to not have myself attached to anyone

I've made mean face, said fucked up phrases

Gone more and more days without shaving

Picked up more weight, dressed to NOT impress

All in attempts to get no attention

But here you come again… at this time

The pessimist in me begs you to do something stupid and thoughtless

Just so I have a reason to not gravitate to you

Something that will make me feel uncomfortable

Do something so horrible that it makes me dig up the roots your growing in me

Be superficial or closed-minded

Lie about something

And the fact that you don't pisses me off

Even the pessimist in me must sway to you..

Please forget to text me when you get home

Letter One

Dear you,

I am trying patience, but it almost feels like if I did not want it, you would want it. If I did not try, you would try. If I say fuck it, you would want to love it in the worst way. I do not want you to be mad at me for feeling this way. You say that it has nothing to do with me, but it is me. Maybe it's me that you can't see. I can't help but take things personally because I so desperately want to be the person you see exclusively.

I lay here staring into the back of your head trying to see through it. What makes you want to change when it's time to say let's do it and make it real? What clicks in your mind that is different from the serenity we are feeling right now? How is it that you can remain only with me now, but cannot make that same promise then? I almost feel like I am always fighting a battle that I cannot win. For me, winning is not the exchange of rings; however, I feel it is the exchange of ideas and the union of the earthly trinity of mind, body and soul. Maybe, I shouldn't give it thought and just enjoy the ride. I know me and could not do that even if I wanted to because it would come across as being unconcerned.

I want you to do whatever you want to do, but if your mind or heart are in disagreement with mine, then what do I do?

Rescue

I have come to rescue you, but do you want to be saved

When I see you, I see someone who is surrounded by walls built with stones of victimization, held together with mode composed of lonely nights because you felt you need not depend on someone else to keep you company. I want to save you from that. I want to save you from always feeling like you need to be strong for yourself, by yourself only to have yourself take care of yourself. Instead of embracing me, you fight me. You want to hold on to your former life and quasi-existence. I understand that. It is safe.

You have taught yourself to respect that and you have said it enough that it is all you understand. You treat me like an intruder that must be apprehended before goods are stolen. I only want to restore and rebuild you into a loving man who is capable of feeling.

Tears are human....

Letter Two

Dear you,

I used to see so much and dream so much. I used to be warmed so much by you, but now that warmth escapes me. It is not necessarily that you have done anything more or less. I have MADE my warmth cease for fear of not having you near. I feel like I have to cut parts of me off just so I can make you comfortable with me. While ensuring your comfort, I increase my discomfort. Because I have had to love you less than my full potential, I feel my love is caged....inhibited... enclosed....

I can't half love you.....

No Flaws

I will love you

Beautifully

Perfectly

with not so much as a blemish or stain

as untainted.... as virginity

as divine as the formation of individual petals combining their

individuality to form one fragrant rose...

appealing

I will be to your senses

soothing to your body

solace to your troubled mind

as persistent as a lion to prey

I will pursue your happiness and well-being

never shall you be destitute in spirit

nor lacking any need if it is in my means

as faithful as the sun rising and falling

I'll never fall short of my commitment to contributing to your happiness

even when overcasts and clouds may try to blind my efforts

with bitter coldness

with drenching rain

REMEMBER...

I will always resurface

overpowering them

with warmth

with life-giving rays

I'll love you

love you

with no flaws

Letter Three

Dear you,

Being around you just feels so good to me. It makes me rethink the things I did before. Things that seemed to be the BEST manifested before me now pale in comparison to what we've shared in such a short time. It feels like I've known you all my life and it feels like the times I didn't know you this part of me was lifeless. Wandering around like Frankenstein wasting time and money.

I can't say that I wish I met you first, though. It took a lot of breaking to get me to be who I am for you and I'm thankful for that. Maybe one day, you'll say to me that you want to be my one and only, and I won't have to write thoughts of love and hope.

If you needed me to, I would breathe for you. I long for the day when I can say it and not be judged as me pushing or rushing you into anything.

In Your Own Time

Patience has never been one of my strong suits

Especially when I am in pursuit of happiness

Often times, I have shortchanged myself

By accepting less than the best or just one of the rest

Because what I wanted didn't progress

But... you being so invaluable to me

Makes me think you are worth waiting on...

And while I don't know the inner workings of your mind

I hope that you will show me

And so that I can understand better

Who you are and why you are the way you are...

All good things take time to build

And I thank you for taking your time with me

While you establish the strength of your own will

And taking time to figure out how you really feel

But I want to tell you that my love for you is beyond real

And often times, I find myself being less selfish...And more selfless.....

Similarities

Similarities in where you've been

What things you have done

Things your heart has felt

Assumptions of assurance

Combined with presumptions and promises of permanency

But still all gone...

Feeling all wrong

And all things seem gone wrong

Similarities,

That take you back to where you were then

To who you were then

And what your heart felt then

Thoughts of what you gave

And when gifts went unreciprocated

What parts you had left of self

Innumerable pieces leaving you to rebuild, reform and revise

To see things differently with a new set of eyes ...

To live differently..

I don't write about things I know nothing about

And I admit.. you been in this longer than me

So thank you for being caring and protecting

So cautious in your directing of me

But what about you?

What about what you feeling?

Are you doing what you truly want to be doing with me?

Stated differently...what you truly need to be doing with me?

Assumptions of assurance

Combined with presumptions and promises of permanency

Only to find that you were mistaken

Steps away from you they've taken..

And it's left you unyielding to be vulnerable like you were before

And to love anyone like you loved them once more

Evermore or forevermore

But it's you that I implore and encourage

I can think of when the thought of loving someone else left me discouraged,

But if I can have the courage to stay strong,

Then you too can carry on and keep giving it

And because the others were unable to receive it

Shouldn't make you unwilling to give it...

I respect and believe deeply in self-preservation,

Nobody is going to preserve you like you

But self keeping self to self

Can keep you from someone who you deserve and who deserves you...

And who only wants to nurture you and be nurtured by you

These similarities that make think you see yourself in me

Past indiscretions that make you handle me personal-professionally

And past pains that's forced you to manacle your vulnerability

When to me, all it takes is a sound decision

With a sound mind, committed to do right

To make the sound come across the lips, and spoken genuinely...

 I don't write about things I know nothing about

And I admit, you have been in this longer than me

So you have seen more.... Experienced more....

But still contend that you have never experienced me....

Someone kind of like me maybe..

Dig deeper

Because it is not safe or right to make judgment on similarities you see...

25

I promise....

to always tell you the truth about how I feel

to always think of your feelings before speaking

to never take you for granted

to never make you feel that you are anything less than a priority to me

to make you feel safe

to love you the same whether physical things change or not.

to provide for you what I can, whenever I can

to do my very best to feel what you are feeling

to pray for you

to provide direction for you when I can, and take direction from you when you know the way

to make you always feel like a man by letting you always be a man

to never resent the commitment we have made

to plant seeds along the way so that we can grow

to always be nourishing to your spirit

to always be reminded of how grateful I am to have you and to have met you to try to never be selfish, but in the times when I am, man enough to make the adjustments to compromise.

to bring joy and not pestilence or malice into your life

to FOREVER speak only positively of you to others, even if I feel negatively about things you do

to make you my only resource other than God when handling issues that may come up down the road (that's a hard one, but I think it best)

to always have a sense of humor

to always be a motivation for you to reach your goals

to always know that I deserve to be treated well, and you do as well.

to never again look at what we don't have, but always focus on what we do have

to not hold grudges

to always learn to speak your language and teach you mine, and understand that there will always be a difference in our tongues, but the thing that will make it work is compromise.

Letter Four

Dear you,

You don't treat me right sometimes. I can almost seem like you have more fun with other people than you do with me. Looking over this thing we got going here, I can almost see where we missed a few connections, and where I missed a few warnings. You do not touch me or look at me. It's clear to me that you would rather have someone else that fits into your bill a little better. This way, you can see what you really want to see. I am supposed to be your man, but you treat me like some ho you fuckin on the street.

It is easier for you that way. It is easier for you to still not be attached and hold on to follies that could have killed your stupid ass instead of embracing and loving one that could save your stupid ass. In my mind, I am physically done with you. I love the love you give to me, but if I wanted to be fucked, I can find that on the streets.

Chapter 5: Break-Up

I have had so many break-ups and disappointments in life, that it becomes embarrassing to share the stories. It reveals imperfection. By the time the ending of a relationship is made public, it has already been dead for some time in most cases. The break-up is when you smell the stench of decay, accept it and live apart. It is also the point when the million reasons your relationship ended comes to light. Compromises made during the relationship lose their relevance, and one can be left with the feeling that it was not worth it at all.

The ending of a relationship can be a period of mourning. Men are expected by society to not be emotional, to exhibit strength and to not show weakness. Somewhere in our history, shedding tears has become synonymous with expressing weakness. This is just plain wrong and I do not subscribe to the teaching. Crying not only cleanses the soul, it also provides the nutrients necessary for water the soil of rebirth.

Your Time With Me Is Up

You have lied to me

Mislead me to believe that feeling me deeply meant you could see me deeply...

that you wanted to fulfill my deepest desires

explore the deepest places of me and irrigate my gardens yet unattended

Naw...... that is not what you intended...

You are right, we do have a connection that transcends normality

And actually, you are also right that we do enjoy each other's company,

But when will you see a different side of me to see me differently,

NOT.. as someone that I can joke with

and.... NOT as someone that I can just lay with..

For the longest, I believed that I was being selfish

that I focusing on the destination and not enjoying the ride

not partaking of each moment individually

and looking at this thing holistically, that maybe this is something different that I could get used to...

I believed I was being unfair to you by jumping to the conclusion that you just want to lay and not lay to stay....

Unfair to you.... to you...

Unfair to me, that I have for so long dealt with something in which I don't believe

In short, I am saying that Chad is done catering to you..

I am done pussy-footing around the issue so that I don't offend you...

Your invitation to my heart is expired because your manipulation done got tired

I need to do what's conducive for my sanity

And for your future endeavors, I wish you the best of luck

The clock has ticked its last second in our personal endeavors,

And pooh, your time with me is up......

Waves

It's almost like you try your hardest to swim away,

but the waves of this turbulent sea we call life washes you right back on to me...

and when you return...

your lungs are inundated with salt water

and you need my breath to help you breathe again.....

you are filled with poison from stings and bites from the creatures of the sea

and you need the medicine only I can give to cure your tainted blood.....

your body is weary from your press against the tide.....

and you need my hands to caress the muscles from a fight you didn't have to fight

once revived you remember none of this...

your mind creates mirages of others who u think were there to help save your life....

but I was and still am the only one who was ever at your beach...

Self Portrait

Perception is reality and reality is real

I cannot change the way you feel

You are a biased artist

Blind to true details

Your eyes only see what you want them to see

Your brush paints horizontal lines vertically

Serene rural scenes portrayed as busy nights in the city

Opened doors as closed safes with no keys

Evergreen bushes as leaf-barren trees

Beautiful butterflies as killer bees

Why did I let you paint portraits of me?

It drove me crazy to believe that I could be a villain like this

That I'm not patient

That I did not love you enough

Or my method of loving was wrong

Your Promises

How many nights must I sleep alone with you by my side?

How many places can we go together, and I still feel alone?

I live and breathe right beside you, but I question if you know I'm alive

You said you'd treat me right,

but this don't nothing like right....

Now I'm just sitting..

Watching...

Waiting on love

Anticipating that you would hold me like you said you would.

And I'm hoping...

praying...

wishing...

that today just might be different

and you'd invest the time to love me like you said you would......

like I just knew you could...

How many times will I cater to your needs before you see I have needs?

You don't even see how your neglecting me is hurting me....

... how the tears form in my eyes....

the very tears you said you would never make me cry...

Now I'm just sitting..

Watching...

Waiting on love

Anticipating that you would hold me like you said you would.

And I'm hoping...

praying...

wishing...

that today just might be different

and you'd invest the time to love me like you said you would......

like I just knew you could...

Your Paint, Your Brush

At first...

I believed in your portrait of me.

Insensitive,

Insane

and incapable of loving deeper.

That I was only able to love you surfacely?

Superficially? (or whatever that shit was you said to me)..

Unavailable,

Ungrateful,

and unable to see your progress with me...

....that you made every attempt to be close to me

and be real with me...

At first...

I believed in the portrait that you painted of you

Dedicated,

Devine,

and diligently determined to teach me what love is..

that... love is not rushed...

It is not carefully calculated,

that it was my own thoughts (not yours) that cause me
to be frustrated

Mellow,

Mature

and more than enough to surpass any man's wants

to truly see what he really needs...

But if perception is merely personal reality,

and reality is your own personal "real",

then I can't live by your brush and paint,

nor by how you feel..

I now believe that anything that don't grow is dead

and my view of its vitals (and lack thereof) is not in my
head

I now know that our connection should have left under
the sheets we came on,

and not into our lives, respectively, carried on

You may have been enough to fill it till is throbbed at the seams,

but not enough to fulfill my dreams

At last... I see

Lust Letter

I'm not going to pretend that I knew in the beginning that I was going to love you like I do now. I lusted for you. I wanted to know what parts you liked tasted and what those parts tasted like. I wanted to know what parts you liked touched and what those parts felt like pressed against me at night.

You gave me fever..

There was a certain mystery about you that was unsolved, and I could not and would not rest until the curiosity boiling inside me was dissolved. Once I got to know you beyond the physical, I realized I couldn't rush it (though parts of me were itching for you). Immediately after we became acquainted, I knew that I could love you.

You saw things differently

You saw someone else and "that was that" for my fantasy. You left me. It was over. Finished. Done. I loved you no less, but resented you more because not only did you fuck me once…. You fucked me twice.

Lessons Learned from Dogs

1) They care very little for the two bowls of food that you put out for them because that is expected. They will do tricks for treats as long as you give it to them only once a day.

2) They will play with a toy until it cannot take it no more or is completely demolished, then it's time for a new one. There is no toy like a new one.

3) If you start a routine, keep to it. Otherwise, you might have a mess to clean up later

4) They like to be pampered and have their belly's rubbed no matter what you have to do, or they will go to the next person in the room who will pamper them

5) They will show off in front of their friends in many ways: including but not limited to a) Running away from you when you call they name b) Tearing up stuff they have no business tearing up... and they know it. c) Opening their mouth to see who can make the most noise d) Testing each other to see who is the most bad dog

6) They don't like people mark their spots....

7) When they don't know you, they will not play with you.. they will sniff you first until they feel comfortable with you.

8) No matter how unconventional the spot, they will lay there if it feels good to them....

9) They don't care about how you dress them up... clothes and collars don't really mean that much to them in the end... they just want to run around and play.

Sense

You know at first I believed what you said about me

Live my life loving superficially.....

Hurt and damage from the others made me untrusting...

Can't even see that you are the one from my dreams..

But now that I'm out, I can see what it was

I called you out when you were messing up

Damn what a shame

You know you almost had me...

You made a lot of plans that didn't include me

Had me wondering if you really wanted to see me

And when you see me it was like you looking right through me

At the person that you really truly wanted to see..

When you are touching me, do you even know that it's me???

Your body feeling like it is questioning...

No evidence

Yet still I'm convinced....

I'm glad I got some sense

I Abstain

I used to think I needed it,

But now I just don't want it

I am out of the coma

Consciously deciding that what you have for me

And how you can make me feel

Is nothing compared when compared to what I can do for me

And how I can make me feel,

The most beautiful thing about me is me,

and letting the stress you bring to manifest on me is a mess...

Especially when I can digress and have happiness

All by my damned self and without your help......

A lot of the things that bind us are the things that we can't see

They are longer, warmer and thicker than anything we can ever feel

Chapter 6: Rebuild

Rebuilding is vital for moving forward. Being torn down for too long can become permanent. You know people like this, and you have dated them. They live life skeptical of every person's motives, hating relationships and making every attempt to abort fetuses of hope before they are ever born.

I have seen buildings built of stone and steel demolished. No matter how strong the substance, it may become necessary to rebuild again. Though I struggle with building fortresses to protect my emotions, I realize now after having to recover from past hurts that the only thing that must be done is to rebuild. It is okay to cry or even be angry. The most important thing to do is to rebuild.

One day

One day, I am sure it will be easier for me to sleep at night

And not feel the need to have you beside me

I'll feel empowered enough to know all I truly need is in the bed with me

Even when it's only me

One day, I know that I will have new memories that will replace these old ones

New experiences that will cause what we shared to be lack-luster

I know that one day I will have to search my mind to remember us..

But right now, it is in the forefront

And it is so paramount because you are the last one that was with me...

So most of my jokes... Are our jokes..

And my insight is seen sometimes through your eyes...

One day, I will be able to allow someone to be close to me

Without thinking they'll leave...

And I'll let them touch me

Without feeling they are stealing what's yours...

And I'll let them make love to me and know

That the love we make together can only happen because there is love left inside of me...

And it didn't die when we ended....

One day... I will realize that the best thing that ever happened to and for me...

Is me.....

And that you were just a conduit to help me find me...

One day, I'll thank you.. But today will be one of those days that I won't.

Ready For Love?

I researched everything that I could think that may have ever touched me...

And I could never remember feeling love...

Then only to have it deepened when I searched through the verbs I'd use to describe how I felt about me...

And I could rarely say I ever felt loved...

While singing my void became expanded...

And an acoustic arrangement of arpeggios accompanied by lyrics became my own personal petition...my plea...my promise...

My opportunity of vulnerability...

My chance for me to say how I would honestly treat it if it ever came to me... how I would cherish it... never complain about the things it teaches me... and never resent the changes it will make to me..

Because...

Now love lives between the crevices of my teeth when I smile...

Love lives in my vocal chords. I massage it and caress it... every time I speak or sing... and if that's not enough for it, I sing song about it, to it... just so it can feel reassured that I appreciate its presence.

Love exists in my heart and flows through my veins both systolic and diastolic... and it can be measured in the words that I share with people...

Love is the gravity and attraction that keeps me grounded, and I feel it pulling me closer to earth with every step I take.

Love lives on the back of my eyelids only to provide glimpses of itself every time I blink my eyes...and it allows me to see not only in binocular but trinocular for clarity of life... in both the worldly realm and in the spirit realm...

I feel..... LOVE.... I feel..... LOVED.... But..

When it tries to invade my thoughts to make me thing about things differently, I attach chains and anchors to my old way of thinking...

And when it tries to change my vulgar vernacular into something more beautiful and pleasing.. I hurl profanities as I try to revert back to my old way of speaking...

And.. when it tries to soften my heart in attempts to teach me that vulnerability with heart is not the same as irresponsibility with heart... I make my spirit and presence tell the story of the tin man.. and pretend that I don't even have a heart...

I resent love

I.... offend love...

And reject it... when....

It was MY petition..

MY plea.. and my promise to respect it..

To never complain about its changes that it would make to me...

Maybe I wasn't ready

I Washed It Off

I stood in the mirror to do my usual regimen

Neck tapered and lined

Sides tapered and lined

Gave a once over with the 00 guard to make sure everything was all even

Made my eyebrows match and removed every imperfect hair

Shaved my face until it felt smooth

Applied alcohol and turned on the shower

I listened to someone on the radio singing about beauty

And I began looking at me and remembering when I felt this way about me

When the mere sight of me caused a ruckus and a quake in my own soul

When I was caught up on the external beatness

Not looking at how beat up I was internally

As of late though, I have found it hard to see me how I used to see me

When I looked at my face, I saw it covered in boils formed by all of the lies I believed and internalized when found to be lies

Some from others...

Some I told myself...

My skin was saturated in waste dumped on me by bad spirits I have allowed myself to entangle myself with

I turned around to look at my back and noticed that all the roses were gone

And all that's left from all the gardens I planted on my back was weeds and thorns...

And they were digging into my flesh.

Ripping it... And tearing it...

And robbing the once fertile grounds of nutrients

I looked at my legs and realized they were covered thigh high in quicksand residue from where I walked into and out of sinking situations

In and out so many times apparently that it reminded me of the water lines in my apartment after The hurricane

And somehow... My feet were covered in black ash from walking in what felt like hell

But not realizing that it was hot because to me

I was so focused on making sure that

My neck was tapered and lined

My sides were tapered and lined

I gave a one over with the 00 guard to make sure everything was all even

I made my eyebrows match and removed every imperfect hair

I shaved my face until it felt smooth

And then applied alcohol and turned on the shower

Because what you see was what was important

Not what lies beneath

I got in the shower

And I decided to allow the water to run over me for a little longer this time

And as I got my towel and soap to begin to wash my face I could see lies and bad spirits in the water at my feet

Lather... Rinse... Repeat...

And as my hands began to rub and caress my thighs and feet... I saw the quicksand go down the drain...

Lather... Rinse... Repeat...

And seeing all of this, I washed my back with the anticipation of clearing out the weed infested and thorn infested garden...

But as I got down a layer... I saw sacks of dead and infertile seeds never planted...

I realized that my insatiable nature caused me to try to plant too many different plants...

And I let unqualified gardeners work in my fields...

So now I had to wash off the left behind seeds from their guilt, shame and insecurity plants away..

Feeling clean.. I turned off the shower..

(Hell.. The water had grown cold anyway..)

I dried myself off

Stood in the mirror

And saw precious jewels and stones of my own...

Crystal...Hessonite... Amethysts... and Diamonds...

And I could see my beautiful brown skin...

And was fine with the natural blemishes..

Realizing that being clean is more than what you see...

And personal superficiality is not as super as people make it to be..

Sometimes... You miss things you need to see

Clean-up

My environment is a reflection of my thoughts....

It's funny how one thing on top of another thing can get messy

... and if you don't clean up as you go, you'll end up like...

well... like someone I know....

With piles of mess so high that you can't even see your mirror..or see you in the mirror...

You'll become incapable of articulating how you really feel

Because you can't see how feel to form phrases that make sense...

Your soul will give your body every indication that it is crying

but you won't see that your eyes haven't shed one tear...

Your voice will be so tired from yelling for help

but you won't be able to see that your lips haven't parted and you ain't said shit...

You'll think that everyone you've ever loved has abandoned you...

and though some of them have, you won't see who's left....

Because your world is a mess... and your thoughts are a mess....

You will begin to hoard all the things you can touch

because the tangible makes you feel secure...

and the intangible makes you feel insecure because it cannot be seen

faith becomes lost in a pile of shit that you should just throw away....

Because it's making your world a mess..

cluttering your thoughts making them messy and thereby a mess...

And there are no words that can express or explain what a mess is

Hell, you barely know what's in it...

How do you classify a rattail comb or two, couple of phone chargers, an old love letter, a notebook full of rants that you wrote down, some pants you can't fit, a shirt you hate, a candy wrapper, $3.59 worth of change and an unopened box of razor blades

None of that goes together logically...

but each represents at least one unprocessed emotion and some are just jam packed with emotions

My friends before you become like... well...this person I know..

I got two words..... clean up...

I did..

Had to.

Pruned

Dear God,

As I grow to know more of you and become aware of things that you would have me to do, I realize it is true that your ways are not my ways, and you are the head of my life. But I got control issues. I have to know what's going on and why are things going on. And, if I don't like it I will ask: Can we do something else? Is there any other way that this can be done? It is not my intention to question you at all, because questioning can sound like doubt, and that is not what this is about. I just need more information sometimes.

I have begun praying harder about me, and battling my own demons. And Lord, it seems as SOON as I my faith increased my world changed. Everything I was even a month ago, is not who I am today. The world that I had grown accustomed to is now changed. Lord, I got to change where I worship. And I am sitting here at 4:44AM on a random Tuesday with 4 days left in this barren city (to me anyway) wondering why do I have to leave here?? Why the change? You heard me Lord!!!! I was waging warfare against the enemies and his allies that are out to accuse me and kill me.... but now you letting them slay me??

SO... in efforts to make myself feel I was in control again, I tried to venture off. Allowed my mind to think of worldly things and chase after the pleasure of my flesh, but all attempts have failed... I have not been able to FULLY enjoy social functions I used to enjoy because I felt convicted..... I cannot allow myself to even begin to think about enjoying things I used to enjoy because those feelings become arrested.... I have searched from one end of the world (as I know it) to the other end of it in order to fill the voids that I feel, but still to only feel unsatisfied and all the more empty.

And then it came to me: There is no club, cocktail, church or concubine that will be able to fill the place that You need to reside. Even the most BEAUTIFUL roses of the bush have to be cut so that more will grow. Now I give up.... and "shut up" (thanks pastor clay)..... I accept my pruning so that I can grow stronger in the spirit.... and learn more of You.. and experience You for who You are....

God, whatever You have for me it is for me. There is no Devil or adversary that can steal it from me.. My faith is in You, and I now know that you will only tell me no out of protection.

www.ingramcontent.com/pod-product-compliance
Lightning Source LLC
Chambersburg PA
CBHW070521030426
42337CB00016B/2057